Treehouses

T0258341

A Methuen Modern Play

First published in Great Britain in 2000 by
Methuen Publishing Limited
11-12 Buckingham Gate
London SW1E 6LB

www.methuen.co.uk

Methuen Publishing Limited Reg. No. 3543167

ISBN 0 413 75380 8

A CIP catalogue record for this book is available at the British Library

Typeset by MATS, Southend-on-Sea, Essex
Transferred to digital printing 2005

Caution

Treehouses

by Elizabeth Kuti

Methuen Drama

Characters

Eva, *about 30*
Old Magda, *in her 70s*
Young Magda, *the same woman, about 18*
Stephen, *in his 20s*
Boy, *about 15 or 16*
Ger, *middle-aged.*

Setting

The action of the play unfolds in several different locations simultaneously, so the playing space needs to be very open and versatile.

Eva's story takes place now in the garden of her father's house. There is a tree and in the tree the remains of what was once a treehouse.

Old Magda's story takes place now in a residential home for the elderly.

Young Magda, **Stephen** and the **Boy** are playing out a story which is being filtered through **Old Magda**'s memory – so although it is set on a small farm somewhere in middle Europe about fifty years ago, these details need not be precise or naturalistically portrayed.

Language

English is not **Old Magda**'s first language, and she therefore speaks with an accent and makes grammatical errors. However, when **Young Magda**, **Stephen** and the **Boy** speak, we understand that they are speaking the language of their homeland and therefore they need not speak with a 'foreign' accent.

Part One

Building

Darkness.

Thin shafts of dawn light slowly rise, falling across and revealing the charred remains of a treehouse in the branches of an apple tree.

Light falls to reveal **Eva** *standing staring up at the treehouse. She wears black and is holding a notebook and pencil.*

In another area on stage, the same dawn light comes up to reveal **Old Magda** *sleeping in her chair.*

Eva   it's the little things of course always the little things that get you unguarded moments which survive for some mysterious reason just snapshots a boring day a trivial act bringing crisps and orange juice out from a pub to you in a car park or a tired look on his face one night trying to make the video work or some terrible joke he made and found hilarious just sitting on the grass in summer with a beer and the day was full of bees and pollen little things little things make it real make his death so so

As **Eva** *speaks light comes up on* **Young Magda** *kissing the* **Boy** *on the mouth.*

and then there's all the packing and the sorting and the cards and the flowers and all the best clothes and what do you wear on this day this day which promises to be hot you can see it from the haze the grass is wet and smells sweet smells of summer death in the summer the birds still sing that's what they say isn't it the birds still sing fuck them the world still so beautiful full of pleasures full of full
so strange the way you're on this rollercoaster one minute all fine ringing the caterers grown up and will there be sausage rolls yes please and wine and jelly and why not must eat must drink it's what you do and then next minute there's that time when you said some bitch of a thing some hateful thing and he

poured whisky in his glass and laughed that horrible laugh he did when he was hurt and it's like dad I'm sorry I don't know why I sorry I'm sorry but

Eva *consults her notepad.*

I would like to say a few words about my father
I would like to say a few words

Old Magda *wakes up with a start.* **Young Magda** *and the* **Boy** *disappear into darkness.*

Old Magda (*eyes snap open – she wakes with beating heart*)   That kiss. That kiss. It will not leave me alone. Forgive me. Forgive me. I am too old to be dreaming of such things. But today – it struggles, this kiss, it shouts, it will not lie down.
The dawn it is so clear today. Just a pale sliver of moon, a summer moon, so tiny, like the paring of a fingernail or a –

Eva   A thumbnail moon we called it not a crescent but a thumbnail – I can see the moon! I can see the moon! even though it was day – (*Covers up the moon with her thumb.*) Do you remember that day daddy?

Old Magda   What is it you want? What more is there to be said? What words more do you want me to say?

Eva   I want – just for today – to find the right words – if just today I could say the right words –

Old Magda   What words would make everything all right?

Eva   To lay him to rest.

Old Magda   I have looked all my life for such words

Eva   My father was a kind man and he was a funny man and he was full of – full of –

Old Magda   And after all this time – my heart is still too full to find the right words –

Eva   He was – He loved –

Old Magda   Why come looking now for explanations?

Eva   He loved his garden this garden this was ours

Old Magda   Why now? After all this time? Why today?

Eva   He was happy in this garden

Old Magda   It was long, long ago – why must there be words and explanations?

Eva   His garden – mine and his – when everything was ours alone, just him and me, that was a good time –

Old Magda   It was long ago.

Eva   Do you remember? Before everything –

Old Magda   If I have fallen from grace – if I fell – do I not have the right to let it be what it was, to let it pass from me, without this struggle, to justify, to explain. Why cannot it simply be what it was? No more words.

Eva   In the beginning –

Old Magda   It was a long time ago.

Eva   It was a simple time.

Old Magda   The time is never simple.

Eva   The rain rained or the sun shone or the wind blew, each day clean and fresh like a new shirt to put on.

Old Magda   That's the lie of a lazy memory.

Eva   I'd like to remember him that way. Before – I can remember him best that way. Simplest.

Old Magda   Perhaps I was innocent. But still things they are never never simple. Never, never.

Stephen *is waiting to surprise* **Young Magda**.

Stephen   Magda!

Young Magda   Oh!

Old Magda (*covering her face*)   Stop it!

Stephen *laughs and tickles* **Young Magda**.

Young Magda   No, no, stop, stop, oh stop it. Stop!

Stephen   You are so easily scared Magda.

Old Magda/Young Magda (*together*)   No, no, I can't bear it, I can't bear it, stop it, stop it.

Stephen   I'm sorry.

Young Magda   Have you been waiting long?

Stephen   Ages. I was just giving up on you.

Young Magda   Do you want to come in or shall we sit here?

Stephen   Is your father back yet?

Young Magda   He probably will be by now.

Stephen   Then let's stay here. If we go in I can't kiss you.

Young Magda   I can't stay long, I haven't got the eggs yet.

Stephen   Ah. So from this I deduce that tonight is omelette night?

Young Magda   Though there's something wrong with the hens, they're hardly laying at all at the moment.

Stephen   Why's that?

Young Magda   I think they don't like the planes.

Stephen   There were two last night.

Young Magda   Were there?

Stephen   They were really low. You must have been snoring too loudly.

Young Magda   I don't snore.

Stephen   How do you know?

Young Magda   I don't.

Stephen   What's that smell?

Young Magda   I think it's the honeysuckle.

Stephen (*savouring the word*)   Honeysuckle.

Young Magda (*looks at him; draws back*)   What?

Stephen   What?

Young Magda   What are you thinking of?

Stephen   All the things I'd like to do to you.

Young Magda   God, Stephen.

Stephen   Can I not say that?

Young Magda   Yes you can *say* it.

Stephen   What then?

Young Magda   You just shouldn't think it.

Stephen   You're completely absurd.

Young Magda   Am I?

Stephen   Yes.

Young Magda   Sorry.

Stephen   No, it's why I love you. Partly why I love you.

Young Magda   Oh.

Stephen   Now you're supposed to say why you love me.

Young Magda   Am I?

Stephen   Yes. Go on.

Young Magda   All right, I love you because. Because. (*Stops, thinks, looks at him.*) What?

Stephen   This is really depressing.

Young Magda   I don't know why I love you, I just do – I just. I just think you're –

Stephen   What?

Young Magda   Oh stop it. You always do this to me.

Stephen   You never have an answer.

Young Magda   You shouldn't need an answer.

Eva   If today marks an end then it must also mark a beginning – the beginning of how it will be – like travelling to a new country – being washed up on a new shore – you have to learn the language

Old Magda   The smell of the beach. Is good. Is a beautiful country sometimes, this island. But the words of this language – harder and harder to remember. In spite so many years I live here. More and more I remember words only from when I was young, and the places where I spoke those words. My father's house and his few fields with the dairy herd. The pond that was behind the schoolhouse. In winter we are skating there, on the ice. The yard outside the house with the vegetable patch and hen-coop. The barn and the hayloft.

Young Magda *and* **Stephen** *collecting eggs.*

Young Magda   Any more over there?

Stephen   Just the two so far.

Young Magda   How was school today?

Stephen   Boring.

Young Magda   You're not supposed to say that.

Stephen   Why?

Young Magda   Because you're the teacher.

Stephen   But it is boring.

Young Magda   Well, you should make it different then.

Stephen   Teachers get bored, just like normal people.

Young Magda   Well if I was a teacher I'd –

Stephen   What?

Young Magda   I don't know, make it interesting. Do things. Do stories and things, that was always the best bit.

Stephen   Sometimes you just don't have the energy.

Young Magda   Are you a good teacher?

Stephen   There's a question.

Young Magda   Are you?

Stephen   I don't know. Sometimes. Perhaps. Not often. Why do you ask?

Young Magda   I'd love to be good at something.

Stephen   What do you mean? You are good at things.

Young Magda   No I'm not, I don't do anything to be good at.

Stephen   That's not true.

Young Magda   No but – nobody really needs me, nobody really needs what I can do.

Stephen   That's not true. What would your father do without you?

Young Magda   He'd get a housekeeper and everything would go on just the same. I mean, he might miss me a bit, but he doesn't actually need me.

Stephen   I need you. I'd miss you.

Young Magda   But you'd survive.

Stephen   Yes.

Young Magda   That's not needing someone. (*Finds egg.*) Oh. Here we go.

Stephen   Three then.

Eva   funny thing was you used to say I was your only girl your one and only like all dads do except in our case it was true – after she left – after my mum left – should I mention her or not I think not she didn't feature she left for someone else black sheep tough luck
so I really was your one and only and sometimes when you told me things your sadness brimmed out of you and into me

until I was stained the same colour couldn't tell anymore which was you and which was me

Old Magda   So my eyes were closed, all right, I'll admit my eyes were closed. What should I say? I was young. In winter I was skating on the frozen ice and in summer I was swimming and rowing on the river, I was laughing often, I loved the heat of June and the deep snows of January, I was dancing and laughing with my young man – what should I be doing with all these tales of horrors and catastrophe?

Eva   so all right not simple not that everything was simple in an easy-peasy nice as pie kind of way just that I knew what was home – this was home this garden and it was ours from where the house ended to the hedge at the back these were our territories ours alone mine and his no one else

Old Magda   Yes my eyes were closed to some very dark things. Adult things. Phrases only half understood. Dark things. What else is it to be a child? To protect one's innocence, yes that is the child's right.

Eva   safety in that wasn't there the garden that was ours even if at dusk and dawn there were shadows in the grass and bats flew and somewhere in the darkness was the poisonous mushroom and the snake with a V on its head

Old Magda   But there was a sickness coming, oh yes, there was a sickness we would not escape. It was coming for us too, this plague. The lintels splashed with blood but this, this would not pass over.

Young Magda *and* **Stephen**.

Young Magda   I wonder what's wrong with them?

Stephen   Three'll be enough.

Young Magda   Oh no.

Stephen   What?

Young Magda   I just remembered. We have a visitor tonight.

Stephen   Who?

Young Magda   My uncle.

Stephen   What about him?

Young Magda   He's coming to eat with us tonight.

Stephen   Is that your uncle in the city with the flower shop?

Young Magda   Yes, Ernst, the miserable one. Always going on about politics.

Stephen   What does he want?

Young Magda   I don't know. He's coming to pick up the sunflowers. But there was also something about a favour he wanted from daddy.

Stephen   What kind of favour?

Young Magda   Something to do with the war.

Stephen   What could your father do for the war?

Young Magda   I don't know.

Stephen   Urging him to enlist?

Young Magda   I shouldn't think so.

Stephen   Bit strange isn't it?

Young Magda   He wouldn't say. Said he needed to explain in person.

Stephen   Uncle Ernst. Was he the one with the beard that came to that birthday party you had years ago?

Young Magda   Yes, the big beard and really intense. I'd better go. They'll be here soon.

Stephen   I remember that party.

Young Magda   So do I.

Stephen   What were you? Was it your fifteenth?

Young Magda   Yes I think so.

Stephen   We played that game when you had to pass an orange between your knees to the next person.

Young Magda   Yes I know, it was kind of embarrassing.

Stephen   I was so annoyed you were on the other team. I wanted to pass you my orange.

Young Magda   You didn't.

Stephen   I did.

Young Magda   But you were all grown-up and sophisticated and I was all spotty and miserable.

Stephen   I know. But I still kind of liked you.

Young Magda   No you didn't.

Stephen   I did. I must have done. I wanted to pass you my orange.

Young Magda   That's not liking someone.

Stephen   It's close enough.

Young Magda   See you tomorrow?

Stephen   If you play your cards right.

Young Magda *goes.*

Old Magda   Should I be harder on myself or less hard? I have been kind. I have been guilty – I have not always been kind. I have not spent time wisely.

The **Boy** *appears in a pool of light carrying a small bundle.*

Old Magda   The years are no barrier to him. He leaps them and here I am waiting. What is it? What words can I give you? What is there more to be said?

Boy   Magda.

Old Magda   Can I take your things? Can I get you something to eat?

Boy   Thank you.

Old Magda   Kindness or unkindness get harder and harder over the years to judge. There are things we have done, things we have not done. That is all.

Boy   You are kind, Magda.

Old Magda   Are you mocking me? Why do you – ? I have waited so many years for a sign. Of clemency. Of forgiveness. Give me a sign. But don't mock me.

Boy   You are very kind.

Old Magda   I am not kind. I am not kind. I have not always been kind.

Boy   Am I going to die Magda?

Old Magda   I will bring a bowl of salt and water to bathe your feet. I will save you from the fire. I will make an ark and set it among the rushes for some Pharaoh's daughter to find.

Boy   Do you think I am going to die?

Old Magda   I don't know.

The **Boy** *disappears from the light.*

Eva (*sings softly*)   Repülj madár, repülj
Menaságra repülj
Édes galambomnak
Gyenge vállára ülj

my bed-time song the bird that flies away with a love-note in its beak . . . more a love-song than a lullaby didn't know much of his language the one he was born with perhaps he cast it away with his past a room too filled with memories to enter very often perhaps now that's why the words seem as lost as far away as unreachable as you

Young Magda *sweeps the yard.* **Stephen** *watches.*

Stephen   Why are you always working?

Young Magda   I'm not.

Stephen   Yes you are. You're the busiest person I've ever met.

Young Magda   Some of us have to.

Stephen   Oh, so hours stewing over a hot classroom isn't work then?

Young Magda   How was it today?

Stephen   Better. We did composition. But now I have to mark the buggers.

Young Magda   What sort of composition?

Stephen   'Courage or kindness. Which is the greater virtue? Discuss.'

Young Magda   And what's the right answer?

Stephen   There isn't a right answer.

Young Magda   Oh come on there must be.

Stephen   Well if there is I don't know it.

Young Magda   So it's a trick question.

Stephen   No it just depends, obviously – well, I mean, for example, you could say courage but then it takes courage to murder someone in a way. So you could say kindness but being kind is a lot less glamorous than jumping into a river or a burning building to rescue someone so on balance the answer is . . . probably –

Young Magda   You don't know.

Stephen   How did the omelette go last night?

Young Magda   You don't know the answer!

Stephen   It's not my job to know answers. It's my job to teach. Oh yes, what was Uncle Ernst's mysterious favour?

Young Magda   I don't think it's fair to set trick questions that even you don't know the answer to.

Stephen   Tell me about Uncle Ernst and his favour. Has he still got the beard?

Young Magda   Not telling.

Stephen   The beard or the favour?

Young Magda   He still has the beard.

Stephen   And the favour?

Young Magda   It's a secret.

Stephen   Oh come on.

Young Magda   I'm sorry it's a top secret and very dangerous piece of war information.

Stephen   Right, so I'm going to have to torture it out of you.

Young Magda   All right, all right, all right. It's about this boy.

Stephen   What boy?

Young Magda   He found a boy.

Stephen   *Found* a boy?

Young Magda   Look. I know I was joking around before and everything but actually I'm not supposed to tell anyone, so you've got to promise – .

Stephen   Tell anyone what? I wish you'd just get on with it.

Young Magda   No, you've got to swear to keep it secret.

Stephen   What?

Young Magda   You swear you won't tell anyone else? Seriously?

Stephen   This is so intriguing. All right. I swear. Come on. What boy?

Young Magda   My uncle found this boy, he was hiding, he escaped a deportation. So my uncle let him hide in the store-cupboard above the shop.

Stephen   He didn't report him?

Young Magda   No.

Stephen   All right.

Young Magda   And so this boy's been hiding above the shop for quite a few weeks –

Stephen   In the store-cupboard?

Young Magda   Yes, but my aunt is getting nervous so Ernst wants us to let him come here.

Stephen   Here?

Young Magda   Yes. He's coming tomorrow night.

Stephen   What are you going to do with him?

Young Magda   Well there's more space. It's less dangerous for us.

Stephen   You're going to hide him?

Young Magda   Yes.

Stephen   My God. How long for?

Young Magda   You mustn't say anything about this to anyone.

Stephen   And your father agreed to this?

Young Magda   Yes.

Stephen   How long would he be here for?

Young Magda   I don't know. Ernst thinks he might be able to get papers for him so he could leave the country. He knows a woman with a cousin in the passport office.

Stephen   Hmm. I see. (*Holds buttercup under her chin.*) Yes, you definitely like butter.

Young Magda   Do I doctor?

Stephen   Yes. I recommend several large helpings a day.

Young Magda   Would that be with or without jam, doctor?

Stephen   Oh, with, certainly. Extra jam for strength. (*Pause.*)

Young Magda   What do you think? Do you think it's a really stupid thing to do?

Stephen   Stupid isn't the word I'd've chosen, but – .

Young Magda   He's only a boy you see, Ernst says he's pretty young.

Stephen   What – five, eight – do you mean little?

Young Magda   Fifteen, sixteen – I'm not sure.

Stephen   That's not little.

Young Magda   No, but it's young.

Stephen   And where will you put him?

Young Magda   Father thinks the barn. In the hayloft.

Stephen   A refugee then?

Young Magda   Yes, I suppose he is a refugee. We are to give him refuge.

Old Magda *in the armchair speaks from memory.*

Old Magda   And there went a man of the house of Levi, and took to wife a daughter of Levi.
And the woman conceived and bare a son; and when she saw him that he was a goodly child, she hid him three months.
And when she could not longer hide him, she took for him an ark of bulrushes, and daubed it with slime and with pitch, and put the child therein; and she laid it in the flags by the river's brink.

Lights up on the charred remains of the treehouse. **Eva** *stands below looking up at it.*

Eva   he built it and I burnt it down
my house in the tree my treehouse my refuge
he made it for me himself the summer I was twelve he
hammered and sawed and planed and hoisted. And when it
was finished I climbed up on his shoulders that first time and I
looked up and saw the moon through the branches, just like it

is now, no bigger than the paring of a thumbnail – I can see
the moon! I cried I can see the moon! – even though it was
day
the summer of the treehouse
he was to build it and I was to burn it down

Old Magda   Perhaps I forget how little we knew then. I
don't know sometimes what is memory and what is
knowledge. But thinking of that summer it seems filled with
the noises of flight and exodus, our frightened countryside
filled with burnt out and empty houses, homes emptied of
their families, and trains, trains, trains, always trains passing
through – we heard their steel heartbeat but we did not
understand – I did not understand – not until much later –

Night-time in the kitchen. The **Boy** *appears with his bundle of stuff,
exactly as before.* **Young Magda** *approaches him.*

Young Magda   Can I take your things?

Boy   Thank you.

Young Magda   Can I get you something to eat?

Boy   Thank you.

Young Magda   I made you some bread and milk. Will that
be all right for now?

Boy   You are very kind.

Young Magda   Will you have sugar in your milk? I could
warm it up a bit for you.

Boy   Please.

Young Magda   When you've finished I'll show you your –
where you're going to stay. It's a bit of a walk from the house.
But there are some blankets, and I can bring you things
tomorrow.

Boy   What is your name?

Young Magda   Magda.

Boy   Magda.

Young Magda   Yes.

Boy   You are kind, Magda.

Old Magda   There are things we have done, things we have not done. That is all.

Eva *has swung herself up into the tree – into what used to be the tree-house.*

Eva   today this garden his garden this day of all days it is so full of that summer the summer I was twelve that last summer when everything I saw from my nest in the tree belonged to us to me and him, before it all ended, before I had to share it, before I stopped being the one and only and became one of three and everything stopped being mine and his and became something he shared with someone else and I was no longer queen but minion in some occupied territory

In **Old Magda**'*s room there is a knock at the door.*

Voice   Hello? Hello? Maggie?

Old Magda   Hello? Yes? Who's there?

Voice   It's Ger, love. Can I come in?

Old Magda   Oh yes, of course, sorry, I was just –

Enter **Ger**.

Ger   Sorry, Maggie, didn't mean to give you a fright. I just saw your light on and thought I'd come and do you first. You're not usually up so early are you?

Old Magda (*still distracted*)   Well, yes, but there was so much to be done.

Ger   Are you not sleeping very well, pet?

Old Magda   Yes, but just – I am having some strange dreams, you know.

Ger   Nightmares is it? Do you want me to have a word with the nurse about it?

Old Magda   Oh no, no, no, not so bad as that. I am not ill.

Ger   Are you sure?

Old Magda   Quite sure, yes.

Ger   All right then. I'll take the bin today will I? It probably needs emptying by now.

Old Magda   Yes, there are some little bits, I think.

Ger   Do you want the window open? Oh it is already. Grand. Beautiful day. Bit hazy still but that's often the way, isn't it, these hot days. Now. What'll you be having for breakfast?

Old Magda   Breakfast.

Ger   D'you want to go mad and have Weetabix or something?

Old Magda   Oh same as usual, I think, please.

Ger   You sure? Some of the ladies enjoy their Weetabix, keeps the old strength up.

Old Magda   No, no, just tea and a toast. I'm too old to change.

Ger   Ah don't be saying that, Maggie, never say that, it's far too early in the day to be getting depressed. Just the one toast then is it? Marmalade?

Old Magda   Yes. Thank you.

Ger   Grand. Oh, while I think of it, will I ask nurse for your pills now or will you take them later with your tea?

Old Magda   Later, I think, with the tea.

Ger   Right you are. I'll be back to do a bit of dusting and give it a go round with the hoover later on, soon as I've got the others sorted. Though you're looking pretty ship-shape really aren't you. (*Straightens picture.*) There we go. That's a nice little painting. Not noticed that one before. Is it something special?

Old Magda   Is a town close to where I was born.

Ger   I was going to say it doesn't look like anywhere I know. Have you been back ever?

Old Magda   I have not been back since – I don't know – many many years. Perhaps forty years.

Ger   Forty years, really? Not even for a visit?

Old Magda   There were many changes, you know, after the war.

Ger   Of course.

Old Magda   My husband never wanted to go back.

Ger   Well, that's understandable, I suppose.

Old Magda   But I am missing it sometimes. I wish I had gone to visit even. Is too late now, I think.

Ger   Travelling gets a bit much doesn't it, when you're older.

Old Magda   Yes. I don't want anymore.

Ger   I could give that frame a bit of a polish if you like. Shine it up a bit. What do you think?

Old Magda   That would be very nice.

Ger   Right then. Tea and toast it is. I'd better go and get on with it or you'll all be dead with hunger by the time I get back.

Old Magda   Thank you.

Ger   Won't be long.

Exit **Ger**.

The **Boy** *standing in the hayloft of the barn, staring up through the skylight, moonlight pouring onto him.* **Old Magda** *watches him.*

Young Magda *climbs up to join the* **Boy** *bringing a bucket with her.*

Young Magda   Here we go. Sorry that took ages, it was buried under loads of rubbish. (*Puts bucket down.*) I know it's a bit of a mess but it was all we could think of. I mean, my father thought it would be the best – place for you. Not much of a view. Just sky. I expect you're used to having more to look at, living in the city.

Anyway, At least it's summer. Otherwise you'd have the cows for company downstairs. I hope you'll be all right up here. I can bring more blankets tomorrow if you're not warm enough. It might be a bit scratchy – perhaps if you put a blanket down folded over and then another one on top. I do the milking at six, so I can bring you things then. Breakfast, or whatever. The bucket's over there. For you to – . . . It'll have to be emptied. I mean I can do it in the mornings.

Sleep well, then. I'll see you tomorrow.

Boy   Thank you.

Young Magda *leaves.*

Eva *in the tree.*

At some point during the following speech, the **Boy** *turns away from the skylight, and begins to undress.*

Eva   he was a man full of silences
lots of gaps between us never quite leapt
his loneliness – our loneliness – it was a skin coating the
surface of our lives a dust that got everywhere and settled
there for so long it became invisible to both of us
the treehouse was a refuge, an ark nothing to see but leaves
and sky nothing to hear but birds and the breath of the wind
a place to be nothing in
a place for being nothing

The **Boy** *finishes undressing. The light on him fades as he gets into bed.*

Young Magda *early in the morning comes towards the barn carrying a basket of food.* **Young Magda** *climbs up to the hayloft. Sees the* **Boy** *is still asleep. She sits, watches him for a moment. Sees his clothes. Touches them. Picks them up. Sniffs them. Goes back down the ladder taking the clothes with her.*

Young Magda (*sings*)   Fly away, oh sweet bird, fly
To Menasag so far from here,
Find my sweet beloved
And whisper these words in her ear.

> Take my letter, oh dearest dove
> To my father so far away
> To my mother's waiting hands
> To where my loved one pines away.

Enter **Stephen**.

Stephen   Hullo there, milkmaid.

Young Magda   Hullo there, teacher.

Stephen   What's that in your basket there little girl? Looks good.

Young Magda   It's not for me.

Stephen   Oh well thank you very much then.

Young Magda   It's not for you either.

Stephen   Oh I see. He's here then, is he? The new arrival?

Young Magda   He got here last night.

Stephen   How did he get here?

Young Magda   He must have walked for days. Ernst gave him a lift some of the way in the cart and then I think he walked the rest.

Stephen   And?

Young Magda   And what?

Stephen   What's he like?

Young Magda   I don't know, he's just a boy. I don't know. A city boy. But polite, you know. He's filthy. He must have come through the forest. His feet are all bloody.

Stephen   A polite city boy. And will he require breakfast in bed every morning?

Young Magda   He's still asleep.

Stephen   A whole egg to himself.

Young Magda   He looks like he hasn't eaten properly in ages. Or slept either. I found an egg, I thought why not.

Stephen   Poor little bastard.

Young Magda   You're up very early.

Stephen   Books to mark. And it's algebra day. God, I hate algebra day. I should cancel it, take the brats on a fishing trip or something.

Young Magda   Oh. Imagine. Imagine me sitting here talking to the teacher, and him talking about cancelling school. Go on, then, do it, cancel it, why don't you?

Stephen   Don't tempt me.

Young Magda   Go on, do. You should. I dare you.

Stephen   Now listen here young lady, you're a very, very bad influence and I should tell your father –

Young Magda   Oh go on, you should, you want to, you know you do, send them all home –

Stephen   I should tell your father what an extremely wicked, disgraceful, desirable daughter he has who needs a very stern talking to –

Young Magda   Just tell them all to go home and never mind their lessons till the summer's over –

Stephen   A very stern talking to about what the proper attitudes are –

Young Magda   Oh attitudes, yes, that's right, that was always what was wrong with me – oh get off, stop it, Stephen, don't –

Stephen   What the proper attitudes are towards persons in authority such as schoolmasters –

Young Magda   Oh, listen to you – persons in authority –

Stephen   Persons, I repeat, who may or may not be able to control themselves in the face of – (*Starts tickling her.*)

Young Magda   No, leave me alone – stop it – get off Stephen – please, stop it – (*The basket of food gets thrown on the* *floor and things fall out.*)

Stephen   – of such extreme provocation. (*He kisses her. She struggles, pushes him off with sudden violence.*)

Young Magda   I *said* – get off Stephen. (*Pause. She tidies away the food.*) Look what you've done.

Stephen   I don't understand.

Young Magda   What?

Stephen   I just don't understand this, Magda.

Young Magda   Understand what?

Stephen   Why are you like this?

Young Magda   Like what?

Stephen   I wish – I wish we could – I only want to –

Young Magda   I won't be bullied, that's all.

Stephen *Bullied*?

Young Magda   Pushed around. You know what I mean.

Stephen   I don't *bully* you Magda, how can you say that? When have I ever bullied you?

Young Magda   You'd better go, you'll be late.

Stephen   God you confuse me.

Young Magda   Look. I hate being mauled around, you know I do.

Stephen *Mauled around*?

Young Magda   You know what I mean.

Stephen   I didn't think I – oh, God, look Magda, let's not, please let's not make this a big thing –

Young Magda   I'm not making it a big thing.

Stephen   I'm sorry. I just wish I understood you that's all.

Young Magda   You won't get your marking done.

Stephen   I wish I knew what you wanted.

Young Magda   I don't want anything.

Stephen   All right. All right.

Young Magda   I don't want anything.

Stephen   Look, it's all right. I'd better be off. Don't work too hard. I'll see you later.

Young Magda   Bye, Stephen. (*He goes. She remains.*)

Old Magda *in her armchair sings softly to herself.*

Old Magda   Repülj madár, repülj,
           Menaságra repülj,
           Édes galambomnak
           Gyenge vállára ülj.

           Vidd el madár, vidd el,
           Levelemet vidd el
           Apámnak s anyámnak,
           Jegybéli mátkámnak.

A knock at **Old Magda**'*s door.* **Ger** *enters with breakfast.*

Ger   Tea and toast, don't tell me the room service in this joint isn't fantastic.

Old Magda   Very quick.

Ger   Hope the marmalade's not too thick for you. I can be a bit heavy-handed with it.

Old Magda   Oh no, delicious.

Ger   Now, have you got your doo-da handy? Because I might as well sort out your pills now, hadn't I, before we both forget.

Old Magda   Yes, one moment, I think it's in one of these boxes – I had it here – I was looking for – I was going to ask you – one moment (*She fishes around under bed – brings out box and looks through it.*) sorry –

Ger   No hurry, Maggie, you take your time. (*Wanders to *window.*) Beautiful view this window gets, isn't it? Mrs Nolan used to love this room. Bless her. She said she had lived her whole life within sight of the sea. She was a lovely lady Mrs Nolan. Sadly missed.

Old Magda   Nolan? I don't think I can remember –

Ger   No, no, you wouldn't have met her, she was before you came. She had this room before you.

Old Magda   Ah.

Ger   And when she passed on her nephew paid for it to be completely redecorated. Nice family but my God, enormous.

Old Magda   Enormous?

Ger   Fourteen grandchildren she had I think. Even she couldn't remember all their names. Well, it does get ridiculous doesn't it. Especially at Christmas.

Old Magda   Oh here it is – I find the – (*Passes clipboard.*)

Ger   Oh well done. Now, where are we? Better concentrate. (*Sets out pills.*) Oh I do like to be beside the sea-side – oh I do like to be beside the – now, is that a one or a seven? No, hang on, has to be a one doesn't it? Right, there we go – (**Magda** *takes pills with her tea.*) How's your grandson doing these days Maggie? Any news lately?

Old Magda   He will be starting junior high school in September. And he must play American football. You know with the enormous shoulders. Very funny. Such a little boy still.

Ger (*glancing at photo*)   Really? Nice-looking little fella.

Old Magda   Yes he is.

Ger   You're a very far-flung family aren't you?

Old Magda   Far-flung?

Ger   All over the world. Not like me. I'm the apple that doesn't fall far from the tree. I still bump into people that I met on my first day in school. Terrible really, no escape.

Old Magda   But that to me – I am so jealous to be like that.

Ger   Are you?

Old Magda   Yes, to belong like that, is wonderful. I would like.

Ger   I suppose we all want what we haven't had.

Old Magda   Yes, perhaps, is true. Ger, now I am remembering, I wanted to ask –

Ger   Yes love?

Old Magda   I was wondering – did I show you ever a key, in an envelope – just an old yellowish sort of envelope with a little key, taped inside – did I show you that? Do you remember?

Ger   A key? I don't think so, pet. Is it for something important?

Old Magda   Not really important, you know, but I was looking – it came into my mind – and I wondered if I had showed you and put it somewhere – it seems gone, for the minute – I thought it might be in one of these boxes but my eyes you know, are not so good –

Ger   I think I'd have remembered a key – I don't think I've seen it –

Old Magda   Oh dear, my head is so old, I am losing always –

Ger   Don't fret, Maggie, I tell you what – I'll come and have a look for it with you when I've got the breakfasts out the way, how's that?

Old Magda   Oh thank you, so much –

Ger   Because it can't have gone far – it can't have walked can it. So don't be worrying. Horrible losing keys, I know, I hate it.

Old Magda   Yes, it's just a little one, in an envelope.

Ger   We'll find it, don't worry. I'll be back in a bit – just get these hungry mouths fed. Don't fret.

Old Magda   Thank you, Ger.

Ger   Not at all love. Can't have things going astray, can we?

Old Magda   You are very kind.

Ger   See you later then. (*She goes.*)

Old Magda   You are very kind.

The **Boy** *naked but wrapped in a blanket looks out from the hayloft.*
Young Magda *below with the basket of food and his clothes.*

Young Magda   Oh hello. I didn't want to wake you up. Your breakfast's all here. Do you want to come down? It's all right, no one's around.
Oh, your clothes, sorry, look, I have them here, I was going to wash them, I didn't want to wake you.
You can come down. No one comes this far from the house. The road is that way but it's behind the woods. It's quite safe.

Boy *starts climbing down awkwardly holding blanket around him.*

Young Magda   Oh – sorry – (*She moves and looks away. The* **Boy** *chucks the blanket down, climbs after it, wraps himself up again.* **Young Magda** *still looking away.*)

Young Magda   Are you hungry? I brought you some things. (*She unpacks basket. He eats. She watches.*)
I can bring you some more – in an hour or two. I'll just have to go back to the house to get it.

(*He continues eating.*)

Young Magda   Shall I – I'd better go and get the bucket, had I? It'll probably need to be – I mean, I'll empty it, will I? (*He nods. She goes up to the hayloft.*) I'll bring your clothes back as soon as they're dry, and my father probably has some old shirts and things you can have – they'll be way too big but better than nothing I suppose – do you think you'll want more blankets or – (*She arrives back down and finds the* **Boy** *with his hands*

over his face.) Oh. Oh. Please. What is it?
Please don't cry. Everything's going to be all right.

Boy   No.

Young Magda   It will. Oh it will, I'm sure it will. You're
going to be all right – You'll be safe here – I promise.

Boy   No. I can't –

Young Magda   Look. I'll be back soon. I'll bring you a
bowl of water – with salt – for your feet. I think you cut
them.

Boy   Thank you. You are kind. (*She goes then comes back.*)

Young Magda   Would you like a book? To pass the time?
I'll bring you a book.

She goes. He curls into a ball, beneath the skylight.

Eva *in the tree.*

Eva   perhaps in his head there were all these lost mothers –
mothers he'd lost along the way his own – and then mine.
Perhaps we blamed each other for losing her. But people fly,
they will fly out, they can't be kept, nothing will keep them
and that is all. I couldn't tell him that then because I didn't
know then that I knew it.
My mother flew and he couldn't catch her or keep her.
Once he told me, I remember the first time I met your
mother. I'd never seen anything so beautiful. She entered the
room and I saw her folding her wings behind her.
Those with wings will fly, of course, must fly, it is in their
nature.

Young Magda *collecting eggs with* **Stephen**.

Young Magda   How was algebra?

Stephen   A disaster.

Young Magda   Why?

Stephen   I ended up with a problem on the blackboard that
I couldn't solve and it was very humiliating.

Young Magda   What did you do?

Stephen   Set it for homework. Which means I now have to figure it out before tomorrow.

Young Magda   How many is that now?

Stephen   Three.

Young Magda   I wonder why it's always three.

Stephen   Is that it d'you think?

Young Magda   I'd say so. Do you want to come in and have tea?

Stephen   Magda.

Young Magda   I wonder if – Have you ever read *Gulliver's Travels*? I know I've seen it somewhere.

Stephen   Magda, there's something I have to –

Young Magda   Was it the attic I saw it?

Stephen   There's a lump in my throat and it just doesn't go away.

Young Magda   What do you mean? Are you sick?

Stephen   No. I mean. All I can think of is you, Magda, all I can think of, all the time. I don't know what to do. It's just there all the time, you're there all the time, thoughts of you, thoughts of us – you don't let me go – and then – like this morning – something happens, and I feel you hate me, I feel so strongly that you don't want me –

Young Magda   That's not true. It isn't true.

Stephen   That's what I mean, this lump in my throat. If you could just let me go, I think, or tell me to go, then, all right, it would be over, I could cry at least, and perhaps that's what I need to make it go away.

Young Magda   Oh God I'm sorry.

Stephen   Don't be sorry, just tell me, just say what you want me to do, and I swear to God – I swear to God, Magda – I'm in class and some kid is telling me something, and I'm not listening and I'm calling him the wrong name and I'm getting the answers wrong, because all I can think of is you and your body – and your eyes –

Young Magda   Stephen, I never meant – I never thought –

Stephen   I think we should be married. I think we ought to be. I think we were meant to be together.

Young Magda   Do you?

Stephen   Yes. Marry me. I could look after you Magda. I could be your guardian angel. I could be your rock of strength. You're so young. You're so beautiful. You don't have to speak now. Just think about it. There's no hurry.

Eva *in the tree, sings.*

Eva   Ha kérdi, hogy vagyok,
               Mondjad, hogy rab vagyok,
               Szerelemtömlöcben
               Térdig vasban vagyok.

               Rab vagy rózsám, rab vagy,
               Én meg beteg vagyok,
               Mikor eljössz hozzám,
               Akkor meggyógyulok.

Old Magda *speaks over the singing.*

Old Magda   It was a long time ago. My father's house and farm. The pond with its fringe of flags and bulrushes. The yard with the vegetable patch and hen-coop. The barn and the hayloft. But to say it was simple is a lie. The lie of a lazy memory.

Young Magda *climbs up to the hayloft carrying the* **Boy**'s *clothes and a basin of water and finds the* **Boy** *asleep again. She watches him for a while. She sings softly.*

Young Magda   If she wonders what I've become
                        Tell her I'm held captive.
                        Love's harsh prison binds my heart
                        In chains of cruellest iron.

Oh my rose, your heart's in chains
And I am sick with longing
When you are near me, only then
Will all my pain be over.

Young Magda *continues humming the song and lays out the* **Boy***'s clothes for him.*

Eva   No matter how much I have tried to forgive I can only think of that summer as the summer everything changed, the summer that all I surveyed from the treehouse was no longer wholly mine, the summer I was twelve, the summer I wasn't enough, the summer he chose another woman. The summer he betrayed me.

Old Magda *and* **Young Magda** *sing together.*

Young Magda

Fly away, oh sweet bird, fly	Repülj mádár, repülj,
To Menasag so far from here	Menaságra repülj,
Find my sweet beloved	Édes galambomnak
And whisper these words in her ear	Gyenge vállára ülj.

The **Boy** *wakes up with a start.*

Young Magda   It's all right. It's all right. It's me. It's Magda. You were having a dream. You were just dreaming. Look, I've got some water for you to wash in – I thought your feet – they're really cut, you should wash them or you could get an infection something.
Do you want me to – ? I'll do them for you shall I?
(*She starts to wash his feet.*)
It might sting a bit because I put some salt in.
I wish you could come swimming with us today, it's the only way to survive the summer. Oh. Sorry, does that hurt?
You were talking in your sleep. You do that a lot, did you know? You talk more in your sleep than you do when you're awake.

Boy   I was dreaming.

Young Magda   What about?

Boy   My mother's shoes.

Young Magda   Her shoes?

Boy   They were black. Little black heels. She was walking in front of me. That was all I could see. (*Pause. She finishes washing his feet.*)

Young Magda   There you go. I brought your clothes back, they're all washed.

Boy   Thank you.

Young Magda   All right, well – I'll be back in a few hours with some more bread and things –

Boy   I kept telling them we had to leave, I kept telling them – I've known for ages we had to go – all of us, we just should have gone, I kept telling them, but they wouldn't, they said we couldn't – but we knew, everyone knew. Every night central station was packed with people – we all knew about it – and trains going every night at three, four in the morning, trains going when there shouldn't have been any trains. I saw them ages ago, I walked past once at three in the morning, I was coming home from work in the restaurant, and I saw all these hundreds of people being jammed onto trains. And I looked up and all around the station in apartment blocks there were people looking out of windows, watching – and they all saw this going on – they saw, they knew – And everyone was talking about resettlement then, about persons being resettled in other provinces – but it didn't look right to me, I knew at the time it wasn't right – their faces were – the faces of the people – I don't know – it looked wrong to me. So I stopped and asked this guard – it was dark, he couldn't see my face so I asked him what was going on – where the trains were going – was this a resettlement programme, and what province were these people going to? And he laughed and said don't worry son, these trains are going east and all these people have got a one-way ticket, and I said what do you mean going east, to what province. And he laughed again and said, to another sort of province altogether.

Young Magda   East? What does – ?

Boy   And I told my father this and I said I thought we should go then, we should have gone then, we should have walked out with nothing in our hands, we just should just have gone, we should have, we should have, we should have just walked –

Young Magda   I'm sorry, I don't think I really – I don't really understand what you mean. What's in the east? Where were those people going? Is that what – is that what happened to your family? did they get resettled – is that what it means? I'm sorry, I'm sorry I'm so stupid, I mean, I heard of resettlement – but I didn't really know what it all meant – What's in the east? The trains going east – where are they going?

Boy   I don't know. I don't know what it means.

Young Magda   What happened to you? What happened to your family? (*He stares at her.*)

Boy   No one has been telling the truth.

Young Magda *leaves with the basin of water – the* **Boy** *lies down.*

Eva *in the treehouse.*

Eva   my father was a relentless teller of the truth
he never promised protection he couldn't give
we went once on a holiday to Wales I think, the two of us, a
gusty cold wet and Welsh August, full of sheep and rain and
mountains I really don't want to climb because I am nine
years old and my boots are rubbing a blister on my heel and
can't we have a rest soon please can't we?
And then all of a sudden we're on this stretch of hillside
surrounded by the hugest boulders, all poised, frozen in mid-
spin and we're standing in their midst two poor scraps of flesh
in this city of rock and stone hardly daring to breathe or move,
it seems impossible that the whole mountain should not
continue its wild career downwards, that we should not be
swallowed up in a rolling sea of stone.
I asked my father in a small voice, What would happen if
there was a landslide? Right now? What would we do?

He squeezed my hand and looked up at the grey sky with just one bird blowing across it and smiled a huge smile down at me, and I knew then I had been foolish to be scared, of course he would save me, no mere rock could threaten our safety. So I smiled up at him and stopped shivering and felt happy again and he smiled down at me again, his eyes shining, and it was only then I heard him say – We would die, Eva. I think we would die.

That was before Miriam.

Old Magda   How many chances are we given in love I wonder? Three or four in a lifetime? Two? One?

Under the above **Stephen** *and* **Young Magda** *have been dancing in slow motion.*

Stephen   So anyway what was the verdict?

Young Magda   What verdict?

Stephen   About us getting married. Your venerable father. What did he say?

Young Magda   Well, the thing is –

Stephen   Oh God, you're not going to tell me you didn't ask him after all that.

Young Magda   No, no, look, it wasn't the time last night, it just honestly wasn't the right time.

Stephen   Why not?

Young Magda   He was just all cranky, and I burnt the dinner because I was thinking about how to put it, and it just generally all seemed very bad timing.

Stephen   This isn't your way of telling me you're having second thoughts, is it?

Young Magda   No, this is just me telling you that I'm biding my time until the moment is right.

Stephen   You can change your mind,

Young Magda   I don't want to change my mind.

Stephen   Sure?

Young Magda   Yes.

Stephen   Just as well.

Young Magda   Why?

Stephen   Because if you did I'd probably have to kill you. Or myself. Maybe both.

Old Magda   Set me as a seal upon thine heart. As a seal upon thine arm. For love is as strong as death.
The smell of summer breathes from him. The smell of warm earth and sunbaked leaves, of fruit and corn moving towards ripeness and the promise of harvest. The sickle and the scythe propped in the corner.
The little things of love. The little words. The gestures. If I touched him now would I recognize his body? Would his scent be familiar? Would a kiss be like coming home?
Oh, the little things of love, the little things.

Young Magda *enters the hayloft.*

Young Magda   I've got something for you.

Boy   What?

Young Magda   Da da! *Gulliver's Travels.* I'll read it to you if you like.

Boy   Will you?

Young Magda   I read to Stephen sometimes.

Boy   Your sweetheart?

Young Magda   Yes.

Boy   You must be glad to be getting married.

Young Magda   How do you know?

Boy   I heard you talking.

Young Magda   Nothing's fixed yet.

Boy   My sister was getting married

Young Magda   Is she? I mean –

Boy   You must be very happy.

Young Magda   Yes I am. (*Pause.*) Will you go back – when the war's over?

Boy   Back where?

Young Magda   Back to your home. Where you used to live.

Boy   I don't know.

Young Magda   How old is she, your sister?

Boy   About your age.

Young Magda   I'd love to know something about your family. Or where you used to live.

Boy   Why?

Young Magda   Not if you don't want to – but – I'd like to know.

Boy   Would you?

Young Magda   Yes.

Boy   All right. I lived in a house on the north side of the river.

Young Magda   The hilly side?

Boy   Yes. And upstairs was where granny lived – well she's not really our granny but we call her that anyway – but she always lived in that house. And downstairs there's my room. Katia and me share it. And next door is the big room with my parents' bed in it. The kitchen opens off it. And in the main room there's the fireplace with my mother's chair next to it and beside that there are two hooks in the wall where my father hangs up his violin.

Young Magda   He plays the violin?

Boy   Not much now. It used to be his job though. He played in the picture-house.

Young Magda   For the movies?

Boy   He was the accompanist. Up on the little podium, doing all the tearjerkers.

Young Magda   How wonderful.

Boy   Before the talkies. They had to close down in the end because they couldn't afford to change all their equipment and no one wanted to see the old films.

Young Magda   I love the movies. I've only been three times though,

Boy   I used to see everything. But then it closed and my father got a job in the factory. So we didn't go so much.

Young Magda   But he still plays?

Boy   Sunday nights sometimes. (*Pause.*)

Young Magda   I hope I haven't upset you.

Boy   Do you have to go straight away?

Young Magda   No. I can stay.

Boy   Will you read me a bit of this?

Young Magda   You want me to?

Boy   Yes please.

Young Magda   All right. (*Reads.*) 'Chapter One. The author giveth some account of himself and family, his first inducements to travel. He is shipwrecked and swims for his life, gets safe on shore in the country of –' (*Her voice fades down.*)

Old Magda   How many chances are we given in love? Three or four in a lifetime? Two? One?

Eva   a day in July that was the beginning of the end a day of muggy July heat and I'm in the treehouse for no particular reason and the minutes or hours slide by slowly or quickly, it doesn't matter which and I'm thinking idly about Kevin in my

class and why boys can make farting noises with a wet hand in
their armpit and girls often can't –
and then I see my father standing at the fence talking to a
neighbour, a woman with orange lipstick and dark curly hair,
and she throws her head back and laughs and my father is
smiling with his head tilted very slightly to one side, in a way
he hasn't done for years, not since –
I stand very still and crane my ears to hear what they are
saying but all I can hear is the clack and trill of her voice and
she's all long fingernails and orange lips and she's laughing
and laughing and just as they're about to swing in my
direction I duck down quick as a flash under the treehouse
window so they won't see me, but I carry on looking through a
crack in one of the planks, I carry on watching them –

Stephen *crosses the yard looking for* **Young Magda**.

Stephen   Magda? Magda! Are you coming for a swim?
Where are you? Are you hiding?

Young Magda *up in the treehouse is reading to the* **Boy**. *She hears*
Stephen *and stops reading.*

Young Magda   I said we'd meet for a swim. I'll catch him
up later.

Eva   And later we're having our tea in front of the telly and
he mentions quite casually that we have a new neighbour and
she's called Miriam, a single lady, she's just moved in, and she
might come round tomorrow, just a neighbourly visit, to say
hello and have a cup of tea. Oh really, I say. She seems very
nice, he says. Oh really, I say, can I watch the Muppets? She'd
love to meet you, he says. Oh really, I say, funny name
Miriam.

Old Magda   Set me as a seal upon thine heart, as a seal
upon thine arm; for love is as strong as death; jealousy as cruel
as the grave.

Stephen   Magda! Where are you? All right I'm going to
count to ten and then I'm going to give up on you. One. Two.
Three . . .

Old Magda   I'm here – I'm up here – what is it?

Stephen   Four. Five. Six . . .

There is a knock at **Old Magda***'s door.*

Ger (*off*)   Maggie! Maggie!

Stephen   Seven. Eight . . .

Old Magda   What is it?

Stephen   Nine. Ten. All right that's it, I'm off.

Old Magda   I was only bringing him his breakfast. That was all.

Ger (*off*)   Maggie! Are you all right?

Old Magda   Love is strong as death; jealousy cruel as the grave.

Ger   Can I come in Maggie?

Old Magda   Yes!

Enter **Ger** – *the lights go down on* **Stephen**.

Ger   I was just popping back to see about that thing you lost –

Old Magda   Yes, that's right, just an old thing – a key inside an envelope –

Ger   Key to your heart, eh? Let's see now.

Old Magda   Of no importance really.

Ger   When did you last see it?

Old Magda   I last saw it – when did I? – it was –

Lights come up again on **Stephen** – *now kissing* **Young Magda***'s neck. The light isolates them and the gesture is one we will recognize when it is repeated later. He finds something round her neck.*

Stephen   What's this?

Old Magda   Of no importance really.

Young Magda   Nothing.

Old Magda   Just a little key.

Young Magda   Nothing at all.

Stephen   Someone gave it to you?

Old Magda   Someone gave it to me.

Young Magda   Someone said to keep it.

Stephen   Who?

Old Magda   A long time ago.

Young Magda   It's just a key.

Stephen   Key to what?

Ger   When did you last see it, Maggie?

Old Magda   I think was in this box – here – one of these under the bed –

Ger   Is this the one?

Old Magda   Yes, but I looked through and couldn't find it –

Ger   Oh, your photographs –

Old Magda   Old things, you know – all kinds of rubbish –

Ger   Have you had a good sort through?

Old Magda   Yes, I think I went through – pretty carefully –

Ger   Well let's have a quick look through – you never know, perhaps it's lurking here and you missed it somehow. Things walk, you know, and then they come back.

Old Magda   I don't know why I am thinking of it really so much.

Stephen *and* **Young Magda** *again.*

Stephen   What's this?

Young Magda   Nothing.

Old Magda   Nothing of any real importance.

Creaky violin music from a single instrument.

Eva *sits as though in cinema, light flickering on her face. The violin music becomes passionate, dramatic.*

Eva   I admit I will admit they tried very hard to be nice incredibly hard really there was a lot of niceness not from me though no way
Miriam suggested a movie – something Eva would like – I suppose it was a kind of a date. I got to choose the film. For some reason they were showing all these old David Lean films at our local cinema and I said I wanted to see *Brief Encounter*. You looked doubtful but Miriam said it was a classic and congratulated me on my taste.
(*Mimics Celia Johnson.*) Oh I'm so teddibly teddibly unheppy. So was Miriam by the looks of things. I sat in the middle. I don't think either you or she saw the funny side

Violin continues.

Stephen *meets* **Young Magda** *hurrying towards the barn.*

Young Magda   Stephen!

Stephen   Hullo milkmaid. Long time no see. Have you done it yet?

Young Magda   Done what?

Stephen   Spoken to your father about our wedding?

Young Magda   Not yet.

Stephen   You're hopeless.

Young Magda   All in good time.

Stephen   Hmm. It's lucky you're good-looking or I'd dump you for lack of enthusiasm. Here you go. I brought you some strawberries.

Young Magda   Mmm.

Stephen   Token of my esteem. (*They eat strawberries.*)

Young Magda   Delicious.

Stephen   How's the boy in the barn these days?

Young Magda   He's all right. He has a lot of nightmares.

Stephen   I was wondering why he required your constant attention. Any news of his family yet?

Young Magda   No. Nothing.

Stephen   What about your uncle? Is he doing anything?

Young Magda   Ernst? I think he's still trying to get hold of papers for him.

Stephen   And is there any sign of those?

Young Magda   Not so far.

Stephen   Hmm.

Young Magda   But my uncle says he's got an address for someone whose cousin got false identity papers from this woman in –

Stephen   Oh well that's reassuring then.

Young Magda   What do you mean?

Stephen   Nothing. (*Pause.*) I just think this is dangerous. It's a dangerous situation. It's not a game, that's all.

Young Magda   No one's said it's a game.

Stephen   I don't think your father realises what could happen.

Young Magda   What do you mean?

Stephen   I hate this. I hate you going up there with stuff for him, I hate this whole thing.

Young Magda   You never said that before.

Stephen   I just think – how's it going to end? What if your uncle doesn't come up with anything? What if his family has just disappeared? What are you going to do – hide him for ever?

Young Magda   Until it's safe.

Stephen   What if it never is safe?

Young Magda   Well, what else is there to do? Throw him out?

Stephen   And then there's the fact that you seem to be getting very attached to him.

Young Magda   Well we could just shoot him ourselves, save everybody some time. Is that what you mean?

Stephen   Look, I'm sorry, I just think you should be careful. In lots of ways. He can't stay here for ever, at some point he's going to have to – and if you were too attached to him it might cause problems.

Young Magda   I'm not a child. You make him sound like a dog that's going to be put down or something.

Stephen   I've just been hearing some things that scare me, that's all.

Young Magda   What kind of things?

Stephen   I don't want to go into it.

Young Magda   I wish you wouldn't protect me all the time. Just tell me.

Stephen   People being arrested. People being – .

Young Magda   What?

Stephen   I heard a boy in school saying that his father had seen a woman being hanged. For less than this.

Young Magda   God.

Stephen   Just when I think of you – I can't help it, I get angry when I think of you risking – It's selfish I know but you are everything to me. You are the treasure of my life.

Young Magda   Your sad face. Don't be so sad.

Stephen   You hurt me so much.

Young Magda   You have the saddest clown face sometimes.

Stephen   Don't make me sad then.

Young Magda   All right. I promise. Poor clown.

Stephen   You're such a cruel girl.

Young Magda   You love me don't you.

Stephen   You know I do.

Young Magda   And we're going to get married aren't we?

Stephen   Are we?

Young Magda   Aren't we?

Stephen   You tell me.

Young Magda   I've already said yes.

Stephen   I want you to say it again.

Young Magda   Why?

Stephen   I want to hear you say it again.

Young Magda   I've already said yes.

Stephen   Say it again.

Young Magda   Yes.

Stephen   Again.

Young Magda   Yes. Yes. Yes.

Violin music as for cinema swells.
The **Boy** *in the attic tells the story of this movie with as much showbiz drama as possible. He should be lit very dramatically – perhaps a flickering light to suggest an old film.*

Boy   So. It's the final scene and it's obvious that years and years have passed – and Lena is much older now, almost an old woman and you can see from her face how much she has been through – years of hardship and suffering and despair over the loss of her lover. And finally we see her walking the

streets of the city – a few pennies in her pocket, holes worn in
her shoes – and she's passing by all these derelict buildings but
we can see they're still full of her memories – fountains where
she kissed and was kissed; parks filled with springtime crocuses
and summer roses and lawns haunted by the ghostly embraces
of former lovers; balconies where women have stood in long
robes, yawning and stretching after nights of love; cafés and
cinemas where meetings and moments have been staged and
enacted – Lena sees all this, and as she struggles on, alone we
realise that she's still looking for something, there's a close-up
of her sad brown eyes and they're searching for a face, still
unforsaken, still looked for – a face she carries in her heart and
her dreams – still she searches for the eyes of her beloved, lost
many years but still cherished, still yearned for –

Eva   he courts her he woos her it's sickening like children
they skirmish they play together over the garden fence I see
them share a glass of wine or a cigarette like children like
schoolkids her head thrown back his tilted a little that way he
has she comes over cooks dinner helps decorate brings flowers
and jam she's made it's sickening he goes over does man
things puts up shelves pretends to put up shelves she's lonely
he's lonely it's obvious I hate them he can't make shelves
never has it's a lie and jam-making I ask you it's pathetic – like
some stupid love story in a film –

Boy   And then at this point my father would crouch over his
violin and his hair would fall madly over his face and his
mouth would go this strange shape – on the little podium, you
know, with just this light on him and all the women in the
cinema would yearn with him, yearn like Lena's yearning and
the most terrible heart-rending moment, as Lena searches,
searches despairing, in the grey streets of the city, and she's
reaching the corner, where the café is, where they first met,
and with her last few pennies she decides to sit down and have
a cup of coffee, just one, in remembrance, at the same table,
the very same table where they first saw each other, where
their eyes first met and their hearts first stammered out the shy
and bold and daring rhythm of love – while the music gathers
and gathers –

Eva   and of course one morning it happens, she's there at breakfast, drinking coffee, in a dressing-gown, his dressing-gown, how dare she, she looks up, it's happened –

Boy   She looks up and it's happened, he's there, those eyes, the eyes and face she searched for, for years, long long years of yearning and aching and burning –

Eva   More coffee darling, he says I heard him he said darling how can he how could he she's not his darling, with her stupid brown hair and stupid laugh drinking our coffee eating our toast and her own bloody jam how could they how could they –

Boy   oblivious to all but her lover, come back to her, raised from the dead, and slowly, slowly she stands up, slowly slowly she raises a hand – and now my father brings the music to the sweetest, most devastating, most excruciating –

Eva   I scream that I'm leaving I'm leaving and I run out the door and into the garden hot summer morning but the grass still cool beneath my feet and I run straight up to my treehouse, cursing and cursing, and flinging down on the wooden floor I hate you, I hate you I hate you I hate you

Boy   climax, as finally they touch they embrace, their hands seeking each other's hair neck cheeks eyes, I love you, I love you, tears streaming, lips trembling, love lost, love found, the oldest story – and my father plays out the credits as the projector whirrs down and the screen flickers and goes black, and he mops his brow and the lights switch off and everyone leaves and he lays the violin gently back in its case, till next time, the next showing – God I need a smoke, he says, just time for a smoke –

Young Magda   Sounds like hard work.

Boy   Oh he loved it. People came to the same movie six times over just to hear him play. Especially women. He had lots of admirers.

Young Magda   Wasn't your mother jealous?

Boy   She never showed it. I think she was proud. She always said he played for her. He played best in love stories.

Young Magda   I love the movies. I wish I could see more.

Boy   We used to see everything for free when I was young. But I didn't like the soppy stuff really. I preferred adventure.

Young Magda   Do you play the violin too?

Boy   No, I never could.

Young Magda   Didn't your father teach you?

Boy   He tried, but I didn't have it. I always lost patience. No, I never could.

Young Magda   What a shame. What did he do when the picture-house closed?

Boy   Got a job in a factory. There wasn't much else going. But I think he missed his old life in the movies.

Young Magda   The glamour.

Boy   I brought one thing with me. Stupid really but I couldn't leave it.

Young Magda   What?

Boy   Just a little thing. My father had it made for their wedding anniversary.

Boy *gets out his bundle of stuff.*

Old Magda   Nothing of any importance. Just a little thing. A memento.

Ger (*still searching*)   It's in an envelope, did you say?

Old Magda   Yes – taped inside. I'm sure I kept it safely somewhere – it's never been lost before –

Ger   Just a moment –

Boy (*looking in bundle*)   He had it made for their wedding anniversary and it had the tune he played for his favourite film.

Young Magda   The one about Lena?

Boy   Yes.

Young Magda   A love being lost for many years and then found again.

Old Magda   How many chances are we given in love? Three or four in a lifetime?

Boy   To love and lose and then be found again, yes.

Old Magda   Two chances? One?

Boy *draws a small musical-box out of his bundle.* **Ger** *produces an envelope with a key taped inside it.*

Boy   Here it is.

Ger   Is this it?

Boy   You wind it up here. (*He does.*) And then it plays a tune. (*He opens the box and it plays a tune.*)

Old Magda   Oh yes. That was it. Oh thank God.

Young Magda   And that was the tune your father played?

Boy   Yes, Lena united with her lost love.

Ger   That which was lost will be found, eh Maggie?

Old Magda   Yes, oh yes certainly.

Boy   Do you like it?

Young Magda   Oh yes, of course I do, yes.

Boy   I couldn't leave it behind.

(*The musical box plays.*)

Old Magda   He was so young. He looked to me for protection. And I – I was so innocent and so stupid – I promised it to him. I should not have promised what I could not keep.

Ger   Is everything all right Maggie? Are you feeling OK?

Old Magda   Yes, just a little – I am falling sometimes, being dizzy. I get better now. Thank you.

Ger   Right, well, then, if you're sure you're all right. I'll look in on you later this afternoon.

Exit **Ger**.

Old Magda   To have saved at least one. One life in all the millions. But not even that. My God, not even one, not even one could I –

Eva   to say it was a betrayal is too strong too strong of course you reached for what you loved you reached towards the shape of your desire I was not your burden you didn't let me stop you and now I know I'm grateful for that though then I did not could not know it you never promised protection against everything you never promised protection from the dark from alone from death that was not in your gift

Old Magda   I should not have promised what I was too weak to deliver.

Young Magda *is crying. Enter* **Stephen**.

Stephen   Magda. Magda, what is it?
What's happened?
Come on darling. What's happened?

Young Magda   He doesn't understand.

Stephen   Who doesn't understand? Magda. Who doesn't understand what?

Young Magda   My father.

Stephen   What doesn't he understand?

Young Magda   He says he's got to go.

Stephen   Ah. The refugee.

Young Magda   He says it's too dangerous for him to stay here any longer. He wouldn't even listen to me. He says I've got to tell him tonight or he'll tell him. But how can I? How can I tell him just to go?

Stephen   Listen, Magda, you did what you could. You've done a lot more than most people would. You've looked after him. He's healthy now, he's recovered – he'll be all right. You've done what you could. He could never have stayed here for ever.

Young Magda   No, no, you don't understand.

Stephen   What? Tell me.

Young Magda   Things he's told me.

Stephen   Well tell me then and maybe I will.

Young Magda   It's no good you won't believe me.

Stephen   Well how about giving me a chance?

Young Magda   He told me about the trains leaving in the middle of the night from central station. Packed with people who have never returned. They're taking them somewhere terrible.

Stephen   It's a resettlement programme, everyone knows about those.

Young Magda   That's what I mean, there is no resettlement. That's not what's happening. Those people are being taken off to die – there's no resettlement, it's all lies.

Stephen   Look, there's a war on and frightening things are happening, but you mustn't give in to paranoia. This boy is one very traumatized kid who has been through hell I don't doubt but that doesn't necessarily mean he has the best perspective –

Young Magda   I told you, I knew it would be no use, I told you –

Stephen   I'm not saying you're not right Magda but look at it logically – where is the evidence? How can we know these things?

Young Magda   He said he met a man in the forest like him who'd escaped from the ghetto like he did during a deportation. And the man in the forest told him all these things.

Stephen   Like what things?

Young Magda   Like there was a kind of soap he must never use because it was made from the bodies of his people.

Stephen   What?

Young Magda   He said people were being executed in huge rooms, hundreds at a time and fat from their bodies was being used to make soap and the gold from fillings in their teeth was being extracted and melted down –

Stephen   This is crazy. I don't want to hear any more of this Magda. What man in the forest? Why should he know all this stuff? It's nonsense. You've got to stop thinking like this.

Young Magda   How do you know it's nonsense? Where's your evidence?

Stephen   That's a specious argument.

Young Magda   You can use all the clever words you like but I know who I believe.

Stephen   Magda – I know you're upset, we're all upset, this is all very upsetting, but your father's only thinking about you, about the danger you could be in – the danger we could all be in by harbouring him. He's right.

Young Magda   Well in that case we should have just shot him the moment he arrived, it would have been more honest.

Stephen   Magda. What you're doing is illegal, it's a hanging offence. You have to see reason about this.

Young Magda   It was you.

Stephen   What?

Young Magda   It was you told him. You told him to send the boy away.

Stephen   I didn't tell him to send the boy away. I happened to tell him what I'd heard. It just came up.

Young Magda   About the woman being hanged?

Stephen   It came up in conversation. Anyway, he has a right to know.

Young Magda   I feel sick.

Stephen   Don't be so stupid Magda.

Young Magda   This is making me sick.

Stephen   You can play at being a heroine but there's a point where it becomes a stupid act of vanity.

Young Magda   Go away.

Stephen   I'm sorry, I didn't mean that like it – I just meant –

Young Magda   Go away.

Old Magda   The boy in the barn, he was so young. How old exactly I don't know. But even then he seemed so young to me. He looked to me for protection – well, I encouraged that. So innocent and so stupid – I promised him my protection. All the promises I made that I could not keep.

Young Magda *and the* **Boy** *staring at each other.*

Young Magda   Do you want me to read to you?

Boy   No.

Young Magda   He got frightened. My father. He's afraid I could get in trouble if we were caught. You see a woman was hanged. By the police. My father heard about it. He got frightened. I don't know how to make him change his mind.

Boy   When do I have to go?

Young Magda   He said as soon as possible.

Boy   Now? Right now?

Young Magda   No, not right now. In a few days.

Boy   I can stay a few more days?

Young Magda   Yes. Till we think of something. A plan.

Boy   A plan for what?

Young Magda   For where you can go. Where you can stay. We'll think of something. Do you want me to go away?

Boy   Will you sing to me? That song you sing.

Young Magda   Which song?

Boy   About the bird.

Young Magda   All right.

Young Magda *starts to sing* 'Repülj madár, repülj' *under* **Eva**'s *speech;* **Old Magda** *picks up the song halfway through – their voices overlap, and then* **Old Magda** *is left singing on her own.*

Eva   I always knew of course, knew absolutely where it would go, your thing with Miriam she was to be another chance for you in love, another chance to snatch at life and happiness, you needed your second marriage, I know that now – just – to be the fruit of your first, your reminder of someone you lost, a permanent reminder of loss it hurt to be that to you you must understand it hurt me then it still hurts sometimes –

The **Boy** *has fallen asleep.* **Young Magda** *sits next to him and strokes his hair.*

Old Magda   I am not brave, no, I have never been a person of great courage. Never a virtue of mine. But I remember once I held in my hand – a choice – a key to a door. My life had so strangely fashioned me a door. My life said to me – There is a door. All you must do is go through it. And there it was in my hand, this choice, this open door.

Young Magda   Hey. Hey.

Boy   What? What?

Young Magda   What if I came with you?

Boy   What?

Young Magda   If I came with you.

Boy   What do you mean?

Young Magda   If we left together. I could protect you. I could help you get away. I could come with you. You'd be safer with me. I could say you were my brother.

Boy   I don't understand.

Young Magda   I could come with you. I could say you're my brother and we're travelling to see our grandparents. I have a birth certificate – I would just say you were my brother. We'd get through the border, I know we would. I've heard they trust girls more easily. I'm sure we would make it.

Boy   No, but – don't think about it, Magda – you don't mean it –

Young Magda   I do mean it.

Boy   You have no idea what you are saying –

Young Magda   Don't say that, don't say that to me –

Boy   No, but, it's –

Young Magda   If I had papers and a birth certificate I could protect you. That would make it much safer for you wouldn't it?

Boy   Yes, but – you can't – you're getting married. You said you and Stephen were –

Young Magda   I wouldn't tell him –

Boy   You'd just leave and not tell him?

Young Magda   I don't know. I don't know. He would try to stop me, I know he would. I don't want to be stopped.

Boy   Who else knows about me?

Young Magda   Stephen knows about you. And my father, that's all.

Boy   And you wouldn't tell either of them?

Young Magda   Not until you were safe. Once we'd got across the border I'd write and tell them.

Boy   But they'd know you'd gone. They'd come looking.

Young Magda   We could leave during the harvest festival.

Boy   What do you mean?

Young Magda   Everyone will be in the village hall and everyone drinks. Last year it went on for three days. That would be a good time to go.

Boy   Three days?

Young Magda   We could just slip away the night of the dance – and no one would know for ages.

Boy   Magda –

Young Magda   I promised you I'd look after you. I promised you'd be safe.

Boy   You shouldn't promise a thing like that.

Young Magda   Why not?

Boy   No one can promise that.

Eva *sitting against the tree, playing with the grass.*

Eva   Here's a tree in summer. Here's a tree in winter. Here's a bunch of flowers. And here's some April showers.
Here's a tree in summer. Here's a tree in winter –
I knew that it was coming but when it came it was still – I had not anticipated –
Miriam had been over on Sunday one of those huge boring Sunday roast whatever and she'd brought a fruit salad for afters and there had been the usual chit-chat her usual attempt to draw me out or draw me in – how are you getting on with your French vocab and such like and would I like to be tested on it no I wouldn't really thank you Miriam and despairing looks and angry looks and you got quite sharp with me didn't you? not surprisingly – No need to be so rude Eva, Miriam's only trying to help you she's not actually interested in your

French vocab. – Well neither am I, I counter – well I can tell
that by the marks you're getting – what's wrong with them –
look it doesn't matter, says Miriam, and she looks quite
pleading and suddenly I feel – I feel sorry for her –
– and then suddenly I remember Miriam in a dressing-gown
at the breakfast table drinking our coffee, and I'm safe again, I
hate her again with absolute clarity and I'd like to smash I'd
like to smash the bloody everything all of you and I run and
run and bang the back door and pelt across the grass and
bang my knee against the tree oh God oh God oh God – can't
even climb up, too lost too lonely too weak arms can't pull
myself up can only lie here and – God God God – pant till my
chest hurts tearing at the grass with that dark clawing never
felt so strongly before never felt like that – even when you told
me that time about my mother, how she wouldn't be back and
it was going to be just you and me – even that didn't hurt like
this because then at least I could save you from yourself, I
could be your rock, your guardian angel, your little Eva – but
this time this time is like no other

And you came after me then and sat beside me
said you were sorry
sorry you shouted
and then I had to cry
and you said you loved her
and I said do you
and you said you wanted her
to be with us
for always
please Eva – like a second chance –
to have a family
to marry again
say it's OK

and I said yes daddy
I know all that
and then he cried
I said look
Here's a tree in summer. Here's a tree in winter
Here's a bunch of flowers. And here's an April shower.

(*Throws grass pollen up in the air.*)
When will it be? I said
What? he said
The wedding?

Stephen *and* **Young Magda** *in the yard*.

Stephen   November?

Young Magda   What do you think?

Stephen   I think that's wonderful.

Young Magda   He said not to hang around.

Stephen   Oh Magda!

Young Magda   What do you think?

Stephen   Oh God, that's – that's just – oh God. I love you.

Eva   And I'm to be bridesmaid, in a white dress – a real wedding – my father's wedding – with flowers in my hair – and Miriam's said I can choose it, the dress I'm to wear – how weird, to walk behind your father up the aisle on his wedding day – strange reversal in a way – with mirth in funeral and with dirge in marriage –

Boy *and* **Young Magda**.

Boy   Why do you want to do this?

Young Magda   I don't know.

Boy   You are saving my life.

Young Magda   I shouldn't think so.

Boy   You might be.

Young Magda   I'd like to have something of yours.

Boy   Why?

Young Magda   I don't know – just as a token. A reminder of our agreement.

Boy   Like what?

Young Magda   A thing, just anything of yours. Something I could hold in my hand. As a token. A reminder of our agreement. Like a pact.

Boy   I don't know what – Oh. I know. You could have the – (*Starts searching.*)

Young Magda   Nothing big. Just something of yours.

Boy   What about the – (*Brings out the musical box.*)

Young Magda   Can I hear it again?

Boy *winds it up and music spills out.*

Eva *picks up her notepad, dusts down her skirt and prepares to leave for the funeral service.*

Eva   and the day of his wedding was so – dawned so hot and still and the birds sang just like today and the bells rang just like today and I wore all my best clothes just like today only that day was his wedding day and I wore white and flowers – a midsummer wedding

Old Magda   How many chances are we given in love? Three or four in a lifetime? Two? One?

Young Magda (*shutting the musical box*)   Just the key. You keep the box. Just give me the key.

Boy *gives her the key. Lights fade as she threads it onto her necklace.*

Part Two

Burning

Young Magda *in half-light, dresses, dreamily, almost in slow motion for the harvest dance.*

Old Magda *in armchair speaks.*

Old Magda   They are very soft, these afternoons of late summer, they bring little sounds in the window. Many people strolling along the sea front. Wind brings their voices in my window sometimes. I like to hear their voices. I love the sea. I love it holding so many journeys and so many – transportations. I am like an old bird that cannot migrate again.

Young Magda *is dressed by now, looking at herself in a mirror.*

Old Magda   What a long journey it has been to arrive here at last.

Enter **Ger**.

Ger   Hello Maggie, I didn't wake you up did I?

Old Magda   No, no –

Ger   Oh good – I thought I'd try and catch you because I know you don't usually have your forty winks till later and I've got a little treat for you –

Old Magda   A treat?

Ger   Don't be getting too excited, now, it's nothing very special but – OK, here we go – da da! It's Mrs Gorman's birthday and her daughter-in-law was over earlier with this enormous cake, and I thought if I know Lily she won't make it through that on her own. And sure enough she has two mouthfuls and then asks me will I pass the rest of it round, so here I am doing the honours . . . Maggie? Are you all right?

Old Magda   Oh yes, thank you. Thank you. You are a kind lady.

Ger   Thought we'd lost you to another planet for a minute there, you looked so far away! Now, I had napkins somewhere – where did I put them? Oh here we go – I'll leave you a couple. Are you all right with it there on your lap or do you want me to fetch you your tray? Maggie. Maggie? Talk to me, Maggie.

Old Magda   No – sorry – just I am wishing sometimes –

Ger   Wishing what, pet?

Old Magda   Wishing that the party wasn't so hot and so noisy, it was like an oven –

Ger   The party?

Old Magda   Yes. So crowded and stuffy. I was over-excited. Not concentrating.

Ger   What party is this dear?

Blaze of light and music as **Young Magda** *and* **Stephen** *burst into a wild dance to jazz music. They dance until they're exhausted.*

Stephen   Do you want a drink?

Young Magda   Yes please.

Stephen   You look beautiful.

Young Magda   I'm all sweaty.

Stephen   You still look beautiful.

Young Magda   I wonder –

Stephen   What?

Young Magda   Nothing.

Stephen   No, what?

Young Magda   No, nothing, really.

Stephen   Come on, tell me.

Young Magda   No, just –

Stephen   What?

Young Magda   I wonder if you would miss me?

Stephen   Miss you?

Young Magda   You know, if I died or something. I don't know.

Stephen   You're not intending to die are you? I don't think you should do that.

Young Magda   No, I mean, I just wonder if you would. You know.

Stephen   Oh I'd probably be pretty upset for a while. For a couple of hours at least. Silly. God. I always want to remember you just like this.

Young Magda   All red-faced and sweaty?

Stephen   In this dress. With wide eyes. And your hair sticking to the side of your face. I like you like that. And your lips.

Young Magda   Would you get me a drink?

Stephen   But of course, Magda. Magdalena. Queen of my heart.

Young Magda   Your tie's a bit crooked.

Stephen   Girl of my dreams.

Young Magda   You will be happy Stephen. I know you will.

Stephen   Of course we will. How could we not?

She pushes him gently away. He goes. **Young Magda** *stands in the crowd.*

Ger *offers* **Old Magda** *some tea.*

Ger   Drop more? Or is that enough?

Old Magda   Oh yes. I was probably drinking a bit too much, actually.

Ger   Oh I don't know, this is only your first cup this afternoon.

Old Magda   But he looked so fine that night. Very strong. And – I suppose – manly, he was manly. In spite so romantic.

Ger   Who are you thinking of Maggie?

Old Magda   Very romantic.

Ger   I bet you had your share of romance, didn't you, Maggie.

Old Magda   Very gentlemanly.

Ger   I'm sure he was. Whoever he was.

Moonlight falls on the **Boy**, *waiting in the barn.*

Old Magda   He was waiting for me in the barn.

Ger   Who was waiting Maggie?

Old Magda   The boy. The poor boy in the barn. It was our arrangement to leave the night of the dance.

Ger   Is this someone you used to know? The poor boy in the barn?

Old Magda   Yes – when I was young – quite young – quite a young girl I suppose.

Ger   I think you should have some of Lily's cake. Seeing as it's a special occasion. She sends her love, by the way. (*Offers cake.*) Come on Maggie. Just have a little taste of it.

Stephen *comes back with cake and wine.*

Stephen   Look what I found. You want some?

Young Magda   No thanks.

Stephen   I've got an idea.

Young Magda   What?

Stephen   What about announcing it here?

Young Magda   What, you mean –

Stephen   Our engagement. And the wedding, while everyone's here. What do you think?

Young Magda   Oh, I don't know.

Stephen   Don't go all shy.

Young Magda   Well, no it's not that.

Stephen   What then? Come on, it would be nice. Something to remember.

Young Magda   Half these people don't know us. Or hardly know us.

Stephen   Don't be crazy, of course they know us. I teach half their kids. Just because you're so stand-offish.

Young Magda   I just don't think it's probably the best idea –

Stephen   Are you embarrassed to be associated with me, is that it?

Young Magda   No, I just don't like fuss and things, you know I don't. I mean they're all dancing aren't they – they're probably all far too drunk to take it in –

Stephen   Well then what are you so afraid of?

Young Magda   I just think it's private, it's between you and me. You know what I mean. I'd just rather not.

Stephen   But that's just it, I don't want to be secret anymore, I want to blazon it abroad. I want everyone to know.

Young Magda   Don't, please.

Stephen   What?

Young Magda   I hate it when you – just don't.

Stephen   Sorry.

Young Magda   No it's all right. Sorry.

Stephen   I need another drink.

Young Magda *stands with her plate and glass as he moves away. Fumbles with the key on her necklace.*

Moonlight on the **Boy**, *waiting.*

Crossfade to **Eva**. *Late afternoon light. She is standing in the garden with the remains of food on a paper plate.*

Eva   Strange the way it's the paper plates and sausage rolls and salad in bowls that make you – the funeral baked meats, all of that, the catering – Funny really –
All the pleasantries and aunties and what a lovely service it was and how're the kids and more sherry? and all the time really what you're seeing, can't stop seeing, what you can't stop seeing is the –

(Puts down food and takes off her jacket and shoes, and sings.)

> Repülj madár, repülj,
> Menaságra repülj
> Édes galambomnak
> Gyenge vállára ülj.

(Eats sausage roll.)

> The funeral baked meats.
> Did coldly furnish forth.
> The marriage tables –

Stephen *and* **Young Magda** *at the dance.* **Stephen** *leaps onto the table.*

Stephen   My friends – dear friends – can I . . . ? Just one moment of your time –

Young Magda   Oh no, Stephen –

Stephen   Just a toast – one small toast – if everyone will forgive me for interrupting the dancing, just for a moment to say – a toast – she's blushing now – but I would like to propose a toast to Magda, who has kindly after many years of perseverance on my part – consented to become my beautiful

wife! To Magda ! (*Drinks.*) To Magda. My beautiful wife to be.
(*Leaps off table.*)
Let's dance. Are you very angry?

Young Magda   No, it's all right.

Stephen   Oh look, I'm sorry. I shouldn't have done that, it
was just a foolish fancy.

Young Magda   No, it's all right, it's not you.

Stephen   What is it, Magda? I didn't mean to embarrass
you. Oh please don't look so sad. I just wanted everyone to
know about us.
(*Suddenly* **Young Magda** *kisses him.*)

Stephen   That was nice. What was that for?

Young Magda   Nothing. Just a kiss.

Stephen   You're in a funny mood tonight, aren't you?

Young Magda   I think I've had too much to drink.

He kisses her suddenly and she responds.

Stephen   I'm never, ever going to let you go.

She pulls away.

Young Magda   I have to go to the – (*She moves away from
him.*)

Old Magda   And imagine, he was toasting me, from up on
a table, his hair was quite wild and his eyes they were – what is
it? – I don't know – burning, is it, you can say – and everyone
was cheering – oh it was –

Ger   Was this your wedding? When he toasted you from up
on the table?

Old Magda   No, no, not my wedding, no. It was the dance
for the harvest festival – it was a tradition we were having in
our village – always, from when I can remember. And always
this dance was so romantic you know – people fell in love, and
– it was always very special, dangerous in a way –

Ger   A bit of madness.

Old Magda   Yes. People got carried away with themselves, you know. But he did love me I think.

Ger   I'm sure he did.

Old Magda   And all the time my heart was – Elsewhere. Planning an escape. Oh, I think – oh, it was a terrible wrong. Terrible.

Ger   Don't get upset Maggie. It's a long time ago.

Old Magda   But I was very wrong.

Ger   Whatever you did –

Old Magda   To have such a struggle in my heart.

Ger   Of course you did, of course you did, you were young, it's always a struggle.

Old Magda   But never to know what became of him. To this day. It is like a curse. And still it feels like he is there, in the hayloft, waiting for me to come.

Ger   Who is waiting for you Maggie?

Old Magda   The boy. The ragged boy. I had promised him so much.

Moonlight on the **Boy** *in the barn – carrying the bundle, just as before.*

Eva   in my bridesmaid's dress I am wandering through my daddy's wedding away through all the eating and drinking and out here to the back of the garden, back to my tree and my treehouse – I can hear it all going on, like this, like now, all the eating and drinking only then of course there was dancing and music and joyous toasts and miriam being all shy and proud and my father all bold and proud and look, he says, look, another chance, he says, I've been given another chance, and my face is pressed up against the bark of the tree like I wish this tree would be my new mother not her and would come to my rescue and save me from this travesty of a family, this funeral of a wedding –

and I remember the building of it – how he hammered and
sawed and planed and hoisted and made me my treehouse,
and said it was mine
and when he helped me to climb up that first time – how I
looked up and saw the moon, no bigger than my thumb,
I can see the moon, I cried, I can see the moon!
– even though it was day.
– and the music plays on and there are people dancing –
people from the wedding – and my father and miriam – all
happy with drink and dancing with joy and here am I up in
the treehouse, surveying my colonized territories, my newly
lost country, the landscape of my father's life with me, the
landscape of my home –

Moonlight on **Eva** *and the* **Boy**.

The dancing escalates into a loud burst of joy.

Young Magda *separates herself – wrapped in a coat – at a distance,
carrying a small lantern.*

She climbs up to the barn where the **Boy** *is waiting.*

Young Magda   Are you all right?

Boy   Yes. Are you?

Young Magda   I said I felt sick, I had too much to drink
and I had to go home.

Boy   And did Stephen – ?

Young Magda   Said it was fine, he let me go. He was pretty
drunk. Everyone was.

Boy   I have your bag here.

Young Magda   I'd better check I've got everything.

Boy   No one saw you leave?

Young Magda   I don't think so. No, I'm sure they didn't.

Boy   You haven't changed your mind?

Young Magda   No. I haven't.

Boy　I got scared waiting for you.

Young Magda　Don't be scared.

Boy　I was sure you'd change your mind.

Young Magda　I gave you my word. You have my word. Cross my heart.

Boy　I don't know if this should be happening.

Young Magda　Don't talk like that. We made a plan.

Boy　We might not make it. We might get caught.

Young Magda　We get to the border and then make our way to the coast, and then we get on a crossing. One step at a time. And one day you'll come back and look for your family. Come on, we decided. It's decided. We have to go. We should go now.

Boy　Yes, I know. Magda – Whatever happens –

Young Magda　What?

Boy　You have been kind. You are kind Magda.

From below, **Stephen***'s voice.*

Stephen　Magda! Magda!

Young Magda　Stephen.

Stephen　Are you up there? Come down. Come down.

Young Magda　He followed me.

Stephen　I want to talk to you.

Young Magda　What do you want?

Stephen　I want you to come down and talk to me.

Young Magda　You're drunk, you should go home.

Stephen　No I'm not. Come on, come down.

Young Magda *climbs down.*

Stephen　What you doing, feeding the hostage?

Young Magda   What do you think?

Stephen   I don't know what to think, Magda. What should I think? I wish I knew what to think.

Young Magda   You should go home. You're not in a fit state.

Stephen   Come here. I got sick of the dance without you.

Young Magda   I'm sorry, I wasn't feeling –

Stephen   Thought you were going home.

Young Magda   I am – I mean, this is –

Stephen   I got bored without you. You look feverish. Are you ill?

Young Magda   I was sweating earlier.

Stephen   You look really – you should go in to bed.

Young Magda   I'm scared about you being here, it's not safe.

Stephen   Magda –

Young Magda   If someone followed you. You know what I –

Stephen   Magda –

Young Magda   It's dangerous.

Stephen   Do you love me?

Young Magda   What?

Stephen   Don't say what.

Young Magda   You're drunk.

Stephen   Can you not tell me you love me?

Young Magda   Please Stephen.

Stephen   Please what? What do you want?

Young Magda   Look, I don't know. You're scaring me, I think you should go home, or go back to the party.

Stephen   Even now you're doing it to me.

Young Magda   Doing what to you?

Stephen   Pushing me away.

Young Magda   No, you don't understand.

Stephen   Why do you have to?

Young Magda   What?

Stephen   Why do you have to? Push me away? All the time. All the time.

Young Magda   Stephen.

Stephen   It's not enough. It's not enough.

Young Magda   What do you mean?

Stephen   It's not enough for me.

Young Magda   What?

Stephen   I don't want you if it's – if it's going to be like this – I don't want you.

Young Magda   Please calm down, please –

Stephen   If you're just going through the motions –

Young Magda   No, it's not, I'm not, I –

Stephen   That makes me sick.

Young Magda   I can't help it.

Stephen   How can you say – I mean, what do you mean, you can't help it? Of course you can help it –

Young Magda   You don't understand.

Stephen   No, you're right, I don't, I don't understand.

Young Magda   Oh please, Stephen, please, I can't –

Stephen   Please what? What do you want?

Young Magda   I want you to go.

Stephen   Go?

Young Magda   I just want you to go away. I hate it when you're angry.

Stephen   You hate it when I'm angry? Jesus, Magda. (*Pause.*) I thought all this would change.

Young Magda   All what?

Stephen   The way you are with me, the way you've always been – it kills me. You don't know how it kills me. You kill me.

Young Magda   I don't know what you mean.

Stephen   I want your heart – with your hand. That's all. Your heart with your hand. What is it?

Young Magda   What?

Stephen   You look scared or something.

Young Magda   I told you, I don't like it when you're, you're all –

Stephen   Come on then. Let's go in.

Young Magda   No, I – I have to hang on.

Stephen   Why? What for?

Young Magda   He's just finishing. I was just going to wait and bring the plate in with me. Needs washing.

Stephen   Get it in the morning.

Young Magda   He's nearly finished.

Stephen   It won't make any difference.

Young Magda   No, I know, it's just I said I'd wait.

Stephen   He's up there is he?

Young Magda   Yes, you know he is.

Stephen   I'll wait with you then.

Young Magda   No, why don't you go on – I won't be long.

Stephen *kisses her. Touches her necklace with his lips – finds the key.*

Stephen   What's this?

Young Magda   Nothing.

Stephen   Someone gave it to you?

Young Magda   Someone said to keep it.

Stephen   Who?

Young Magda   It's just a key.

Stephen   Key to what?

Eva *in the treehouse;* **Boy** *in the barn in moonlight;* **Stephen** *continues to kiss* **Young Magda**, *downstairs in the barn.*

Eva   somewhere they are kissing
probably kissing
somewhere in the night
in this night somewhere he embraces her
his new wife
beautiful wife
tells her he will keep her safe
tells her they will build their house upon the
rock
upon the rock of his love
somewhere in this soft night
this moonridden passionate
lonely night

Old Magda   He was above – he heard everything – from above in the hayloft of the barn – he was there all the time – but what could I have done? Still, I ask myself, what is it I could have done?

Ger   Is it the ragged boy you mean? The boy in the barn? He was watching you?

Old Magda   From up above, yes, watching all the time, I still held his key on a chain round my neck.

Ger   His key?

Old Magda   The key he had given me, to the musical box.

Young Magda *breaks off from the kiss.*

Young Magda   You have to go.

Stephen   Why do I have to go? We're going to be married, why do I have to go?

Young Magda   Because, just because you do.

Stephen   What's wrong with you?

Young Magda   There's nothing wrong with me.

Stephen   What's going on?

Young Magda   Please don't make this more difficult.

Stephen   What do you mean – more difficult?
Make what more difficult?

Young Magda   Please, Stephen –

Stephen   What's going on? You have to tell me what's going on. I know you Magda, I'm not stupid. There's something going on here isn't there? There is, isn't there?

Young Magda   I'll tell you everything tomorrow. But tonight, just for tonight, I can't.

Stephen   And this? What's this? Why did he give it to you? What is it?

Young Magda   It's nothing, it's for a toy, just a musical box. He just gave it to me – I don't know why, a memento or something.

Stephen   A memento?

Young Magda   A present.

Stephen   He gives you presents.

Young Magda   He wanted to give me the whole thing but I said he should keep the box, just to give me the key, because he had nothing else you see.

Stephen   So he's finally leaving is he?

Young Magda   How do you mean?

Stephen   Well why else would you need a keepsake? A memento, as you put it?

Young Magda   Yes. He's going. Tonight.

Stephen   Ah. Good. So is there anything else?

Young Magda   Anything else what?

Stephen   Anything else you want to tell me?

Young Magda   No not really.

Stephen   There is something. I know there is. I know you Magda, I know when you're lying. I know what your face does when you lie.

Young Magda   Stephen.

Stephen   Have you ever loved me?
Oh God. Magda.

Young Magda   Please let me go.

Stephen   Let you go? What do you mean? Let you go?

Young Magda   Please Stephen.

Stephen   Oh no.

Young Magda   Let me go.

Stephen   Oh God.

Young Magda   If I went with him I might be able to help him. I might be able to save him. Please Stephen.

Stephen   Oh Magda.

Young Magda   I'm sorry.

Stephen   How can you even ask me?

Young Magda   I wanted to love you. I wanted to.

Stephen   Don't tell me this.

Young Magda   But if I went with him – if the two of us left together – I could protect him. If I was with him I'm sure he'd make it – we could get across the border.

Stephen   What are you talking about? You're crazy – you have no idea what you're talking about.

Young Magda   Please let me go Stephen. You have to.

Stephen   Why do I have to?

Young Magda   Because. Because I.

Stephen   What? Say it.

Young Magda   What?

Stephen   Go on say it. Because – ?

Young Magda   I can't.

Stephen   You never could say things.

Young Magda   Perhaps I didn't love you as much as I should.

Stephen   Perhaps.

Young Magda   I wanted to love you. I tried to love you,

Stephen   That's the difference isn't it. I never tried to love you. I've never had to try. I just –
Where is he anyway?
She indicates.

Young Magda   You're not going to do anything. Are you?

Stephen   What would I do? I could put him out of his misery.

Young Magda   Stop it.

Stephen   Get a medal for it probably. That's what I should do, actually, report the pair of you and get decorated.

Young Magda   I trusted you.

Stephen   I trusted you.

The **Boy** *appears between them, having climbed down the ladder from the hayloft.*

Eva   The tree lifts its arms to embrace the night, the light embraces and is embraced. This house, this treehouse, this ark rides through the dark towards towards towards –
oh the lost territories of love the landscapes changed for ever

Young Magda, **Stephen** *and the* **Boy**. *Silence.*

Stephen   One thing you should know. If you go, I will forget you. I will cut you out of my heart. Don't think that I'll mourn you for ever because I won't. I'll love someone else. I will cut you out of my heart and I will never ever let you back in.
I've always fought for you, I fought to win you, I've always been fighting and now – just when I ought to – I can't do it anymore. I can't. I can't. I just can't. *Exits.*

Boy   Magda.

Old Magda   And there went a man of the house of Levi and took to wife a daughter of Levi. And she conceived and bare a son. And when she saw him that he was a goodly child she hid him for three months. And when she could not longer hide him –
When she could not longer hide him –

Boy   Magda. It's time to go. We have to go. We said tonight.

Young Magda   I know.

Boy   We have to go, now is the time, we said tonight. Have you changed your mind?
I can't go into the woods alone. It's dark. I can't. You said you'd come with me. You promised you would.

Young Magda   I'm no good Joe. I'm no good.

Boy   Please don't do this. Please come with me.

Young Magda   I can't.

Boy   Please. I'm scared to go alone. I can't go on my own.

Young Magda   I'm sorry Joe. I made a mistake. I can't.

Boy   Am I going to die?

Young Magda   I don't know.

Boy   Do you think I'm going to die?

Young Magda   I don't know.

He comes to her and she kisses him – the kiss we saw on page 1. She pushes him away.

Boy   You are kind Magda.

He makes a sudden run for the door and is gone. She is left alone in the empty barn.

Old Magda   And when she could not longer hide him, she took for him an ark of bulrushes and daubed it with slime and with pitch, and put the child therein; and she laid it in the flags by the river's brink.

Eva   And then it came to me – the perfect end for this ark, this nest, this safe place – to release my treehouse to be consumed and exhaled, freed by fire on this wedding night this funeral night even as somewhere new lovers whisper new promises and old promises are burned away or transformed by the flames into new covenants – (*She strikes a match, lighting a torch.*)

The lights begin to fade.

Stephen *appears in the doorway to the barn.*

Old Magda   And his sister stood afar off to wit what would be done to him. And the daughter of Pharaoh came down to wash herself at the river. And when she saw the ark among the flags, she sent her maid to fetch it. And when she opened it she saw the child, and behold, the babe wept. And she had compassion on him, and said, This is one of the Hebrews' children.

Young Magda   Forgive me.

Old Magda   His name was Stephen, my husband. We were
married a few months after the war ended.

Ger   So a happy ending at least.

Old Magda   In a way, is yes, a happy ending.

Ger   Except for the little boy. Poor little thing. What
happened to him?

Old Magda   I don't know. Once – it was years later – I
tried to trace him. But I could find nothing. I knew so little of
who he actually was. It was such a short time I was hiding
him. I don't know if he lived or died.

Ger   Perhaps he made it. You never know. Like you –
ending up so far away. A foreign country.

Old Magda   Not even one. I couldn't even save one little
boy.

Ger   Perhaps it was meant to be.

Old Magda   No. I lacked courage. I promised – and I
broke my promise.

Ger   You don't think he might have forgiven you? After all
this time?

Old Magda   Perhaps.

Ger   Anyway, love, I have to get on. I'll see you tomorrow
with your breakfast. Sweet dreams, my love.

Old Magda   Oh thank you, yes Ger, good night. (*Exit* **Ger**.)
You are very kind.

Eva   so I made a torch of your vows
            as you embraced your bride
            your miriam, your new chance
            I fed all of what we had been to the fire
            to be freed from you to free you from me
            just like today –

this safe place this nook this nest
this safe as houses tree –

(*She sets light to the treehouse.*)

to be freed by fire and fed to the passionate skies

Old Magda/Young Magda   Forgive me.

The lights fade. By the light of the flames we see **Stephen** *coming down to where* **Young Magda** *is lying and embracing her.*

Daylight. Dawn.

Old Magda   Day comes and paints the room soft colours. More and more I remember only the words from my childhood and the places where I spoke those words.

Stephen   Magda!

Young Magda   Hullo!

Stephen   Hullo, milkmaid.

Old Magda   I am like a bird that can migrate no longer. Sometimes I can hardly remember how we arrived – how we arrived to be at this place, with all my keepsakes washed up around me.

Eva *no longer in funeral clothes but in old trousers and cardigan, drags a tea chest across the garden. She begins unpacking it – pulling out old books, trinkets, general junk.*

Old Magda   Oh the little things of love. The words. The little things. The lost and little things.

Eva *finds the musical box. Tries to open it and can't. Shakes it – begins looking for the key to open it.*

Eva   he never showed me this – where's the key I wonder – what a shame – I'd love to hear it

And in a blaze of light we see the **Boy** *as he was in the barn, telling the story of Lena in the film.*

Boy   So after many long years of hardship and suffering, of terrible despair over the loss of her lover, finally in the very last scene we see Lena walking the derelict streets of the city – a few pennies in her pocket –

Old Magda   – holes worn in her shoes, passing through streets still filled with her memories – fountains where she kissed and was kissed – parks of springtime crocuses and summer roses and lawns haunted by the ghostly embraces of former lovers –

Boy   – balconies where women have stood in long robes, yawning and stretching after nights of love –

Old Magda   – cafés and cinemas where meetings and moments have been staged and enacted –

Boy   – all this Lena sees as she struggles on – alone now – older but still hopeful – still her sad brown eyes searching for a face, still unforsaken, still looked for –

Old Magda   – a face she carries in her heart and her dreams –

Boy   – still she searches for the face of her beloved –

Old Magda   – lost many years but still yearned for, still cherished –

Eva   Locked tight and no key with it – I wonder if – did it survive – is it here somewhere – or lost I suppose – perhaps I could get it open, but I suppose that might break it – maybe I shouldn't – what a lovely thing – a musical box – I shouldn't break it, but I wonder what the tune is –

Old Magda   And one day I thought – perhaps I'll see his face in a crowd – I'll find him again – years gone by and Stephen and I long married – children of our own –

Stephen   Magdalena! Queen of my heart. My beautiful wife.

Old Magda   And maybe he too – maybe he did escape, like I did, through all this upheaval, eventually to a safe place, both of us crossed the border, washed ashore and found some resting place – an ark – or haven – and maybe one day to meet a woman and fall in love – perhaps to marry, have children himself – could it be possible? – even in those terrible times – for a miracle, or if not that, then a lucky chance, another chance – at life and love – and perhaps somewhere too a child of his loves him and forgives him for some betrayal of the heart –

Boy   Slowly, slowly she stands up, slowly, slowly, raises a hand – as finally they touch, they embrace, their hands seeking each other's hair, neck, eyes, mouth, I love you, I love you, she whispers, as the women in the audience whisper too with Lena, I love you, I love you, tears streaming, lips trembling, a lover brought back from what seemed like death, love lost, love found, the oldest story –

Old Magda   I will bring a bowl of salt and water to bathe your feet. I will save you from the fire. I will make an ark and set it among the rushes for some Pharaoh's daughter to find.

Although all the characters and events in this play are entirely fictitious, I have found the following books useful in writing it:

Deborah Dwork, *Children With a Star: Jewish Youth in Nazi Europe* (New Haven and London: Yale University Press, 1991).

Jane Marks, *The Hidden Children: The Secret Survivors of the Holocaust* (London: Bantam, 1995).

Magda Denes, *Castles Burning: A Child's Life in War* (London: Doubleday, 1997).

Eva Hoffman, *Lost in Translation: A Life in a New Language* (London: Minerva, 1991).

9 780413 753809